745.592
Ac7t   63520

DATE DUE		
Nov 16 68	Oct 19 '72	
Feb 10 '69	Oct 6 '73	
Jun 9 '69	Oct 13 '76	
Oct 15 69	Apr 28 '77	
Aug 7 '70	Sep 11 79	
Oct 5 '70		
Oct 12 70		
Oct 27 70		
Jan 28 '71		
Aug 3 '71		
Jan 17 '72		

GAYLORD M-2   PRINTED IN U.S.A.

DISCARDED

D1060856

TOY SCULPTURE

Barnum's Food Stand.

TOY SCULPTURE

William Accorsi

Reinhold Book Corporation
A subsidiary of Chapman-Reinhold
New York   Amsterdam   London
An Art Horizons Book

CARL A. RUDISILL LIBRARY
LENOIR RHYNE COLLEGE

745.592
Ac 7t

63520

Oct. 1968

Special Thanks

To Betsy, Susie, Joe, Vivian, Tom, Ruth, Pterodactyl, Mom, Little Orphan Annie, Tiny Tim, and Scrooge; my patrons and friends, Simkin Industries and Springbok Puzzles, Inc.; Paul Smith for the name *Toy Sculpture*; William Blakesley for converting me from a football player to an artist; Herb Kahn for facts of life; my two valued assistants, Perry Hazel and Deric Washburn; Edward Epstein for special historical drawings; Renita Hanfling for the bulk of the photography; Ferdinand Boesch, Harvey Lloyd, David Attie, Sister Mary Corita for additional photography; and, of course, to that greatest toymaker of all, Santa Claus.

© 1968, Art Horizons, Inc.
All rights reserved
Printed in the United States of America
Library of Congress Catalog Card Number: 68-16024
Design Consultant: Milton Glaser
Type set by Lettick Typografic, Inc.
Printed by Halliday Lithographic Corp.
Bound by William Marley & Co.
Published by Reinhold Book Corporation
A subsidiary of Chapman-Reinhold, Inc.
430 Park Avenue, New York, N.Y. 10022

Contents

1. TOYS PAST AND PRESENT 7
2. WIRE SCULPTURE, MOVING AND NON-MOVING 27
   Toy Sculpture Using Found Objects 40
3. WOODEN CUT-OUT SCULPTURE 65
4. A PORTFOLIO OF TOYS BY ARTISTS 81

Unless otherwise credited, all photographs in chapters 1, 2 and 3 are by Renita Hanfling.

1.

Toys Past and Present

Many of the toys illustrated in the chapters that follow are really small-scale moving sculptures. Kinetic art — of whatever scale, large or small — has been heralded by galleries and critics as a unique development of our times. However, the history of moving toys and sculpture is, surprisingly enough, a long one. Because even a brief survey of both moving and non-moving toys is simply beyond the scope of an introductory chapter, I have chosen to explore some hitherto little-known facts concerning the development of moving sculpture and toys and their significance for people of all ages, particularly artists, craftsmen, and students.

As we are discovering in the twentieth century, art can be almost anything. In a more traditional sense, however, art has been defined by the cultural establishment as painting, sculpture, and architecture — with a sharp line drawn between "art," on one hand, and "craft" on the other. At one time, however, the pursuit of art was a thoroughly integrated activity. The artist-craftsman was directly involved in all stages of creation, from preliminary design to the finished painting or ceramic piece, and he worked in many media with no thought of stepping outside the field of serious art. For example, an artist could be painter, sculptor, interior decorator, designer of buildings, viaducts, war machines — and toys. This was true of many artists of varying degrees of talent and not just a universal genius like Leonardo da Vinci.

Toys are surely art, and like any other form of art can be ordinary or beautiful. The first toys of prehistory are regarded by the art historian as sculpture, and not as toys at all. They played an important role in religious ceremonies as effigies of gods. In ancient Egypt, a high priest would literally climb into such a "toy" sculpture. From this interior position he was able to manipulate the arms and the head and even make the mouth work up and down as he spoke. To the worshipper watching this curious, but awe-inspiring, spectacle, the god was actually speaking. These early "kinetic" sculptures were the property of the priesthood alone; ownership by others was forbidden. In time, household adaptations of the large priestly sculptures came to exist. From

Opposite Page
Classical Indian pull toy. Cast iron.

7

these small-scale imitations toys ultimately developed in three main directions: common toys, puppets, and automata. It is with automata, those elegant and expensive toys of kings and aristocrats, that we will be mainly concerned. In the ancient civilized world automata were already fully developed. The rewards of automaton making attracted the talents of highly skilled artists. In general, automaton figures imitated the manners and movements of men or animals. The more convincing and astonishing the actions of the automaton, the more enthusiastic its reception. The high point of automaton design occurred in the seventeenth and eighteenth centuries. By this time automaton creators began to wonder whether, instead of making figures that simply imitated characteristic human actions, they might not create automata that did the work of man. This practical and praiseworthy aim took some time to realize, for until the development of the steam engine there were no existing power sources capable of many general and practical uses. With the change in

the concept of what a mechanical object might do and with the invention and early perfection of the steam engine, the artist-craftsman turned from the further refinement of the automaton to the designing of industrial machines. Thus, the children of the automata became the factory work horses of the Industrial Revolution. Centuries of knowledge developed in the design and building of automata lead logically to the designing of complex industrial machines. These energies spread to many technological areas to support the Industrial Revolution — better forms of transportation, communication, and reproduction — the latter two culminating in the modern computer machines. The same gifted inventor-engineer who once designed and made mechanical figures now lends his highly sophisticated skills to the further development of twentieth-century industrial technology. His playful mechanical creatures came to be disguised as sober servants of modern business and science. The circle has now come full turn. In the beginning, moving toys were of a religious nature. Later,

evolved an ingenious, human-imitating phase, when their functions came to be questioned, and finally "religious" again, when industrial machines became so important that they were viewed with the fear and awe formerly accorded deities. Man in his continuing, unconscious, and mysterious exploration of his psyche has determined that his industrial machines return once again to their early function as toys. Thus an insight is provided into the emergence in the modern art world of kinetic sculpture, the "psychedelic" explorations of light as entertainment (a toy for all), the programming of IBM machines to play games and "draw" pictures, and the awakening interest of mathematicians and engineers in contemporary art.

When considering the hundreds of years that moving toys entertained the nobility — and the masses as well — one can only imagine what lies in store in the reawakened desire of man to make serious toys — now from his industrial machinery. In this new involvement, he will call them "sculpture" and "art." It matters not. It's all the same.

Opposite Page
Device for use at drinking parties. Leaf from a manuscript on automata (treatise on mechanical devices) by Abu'l Izz Isma'il al-Jaziri. Colors and gilt on paper. Egypto-Islamic. 14th century. (The Metropolitan Museum of Art, Rogers Fund, 1955.)

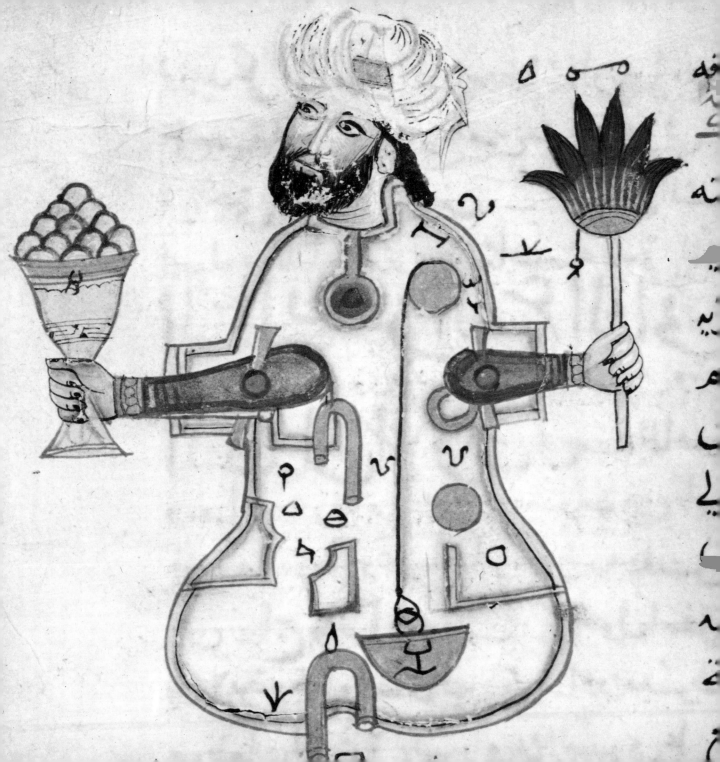

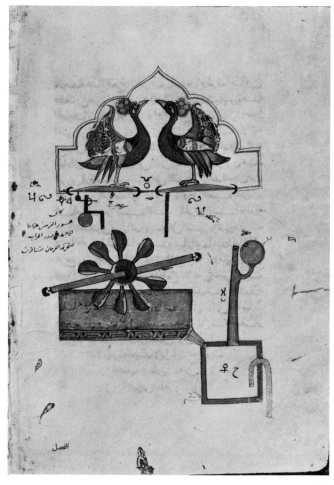

Clock in the form of an elephant. Leaf from a manuscript on automata (treatise on mechanical devices) by Abu'l Izz Isma'il al-Jaziri. Colors and gilt on paper. Egypto-Islamic. 14th century. (The Metropolitan Museum of Art, Rogers Fund, 1955.)

Water clock of the peacocks. Leaf from a manuscript. Color and gilt on paper. Egypto-Islamic. 1315. (The Metropolitan Museum of Art, Rogers Fund, 1955.)

Hound in full cry. A mechanical toy, the articulated
lower jaw being actuated by the rod. Ivory.
Egyptian. XVIII Dynasty. (The Metropolitan
Museum of Art.)

Tiger attacking a British colonel. Mechanical toy with growling sound effects, made for Tipu Sahib, Sultan of Mysore. Length 6 feet. (Courtesy the Victoria and Albert Museum, London.)

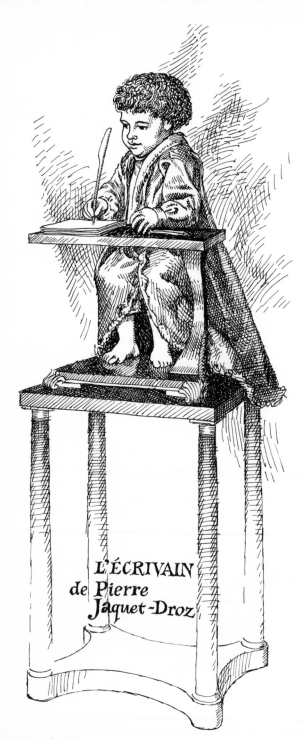

L'ÉCRIVAIN
de Pierre
Jaquet-Droz

Writing figure. It makes quite realistic movements while it writes. French. Mid-18th century.

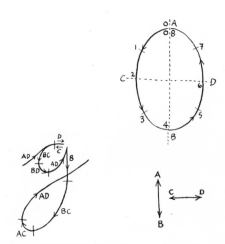

Detail of the hand of the writing figure. The mechanical writer was programmed to write up and down (A-B) as well as from side to side (C-D). These basic directions could form any letter.

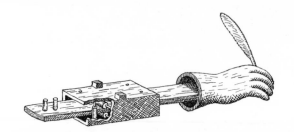

Right. Mechanical device to create a realistic rocking motion for a toy sailing ship.

Below. Spectacular chess player created by a German baron in 1776. It was a great success for six years until it was uncovered as an ingenious hoax.

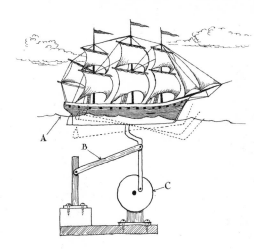

Hand-manipulated shadow figures by M. Cottier. French.

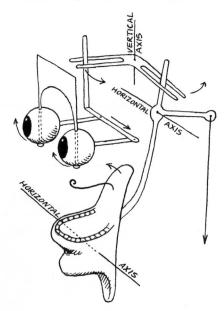

Many automata had moving eyes. This drawing shows one solution to the challenge.

Strasbourg clock. 1350. The remaining superstructure of a large clock, the rooster opened its beak and crowed, at the same time flapping its wings.

16

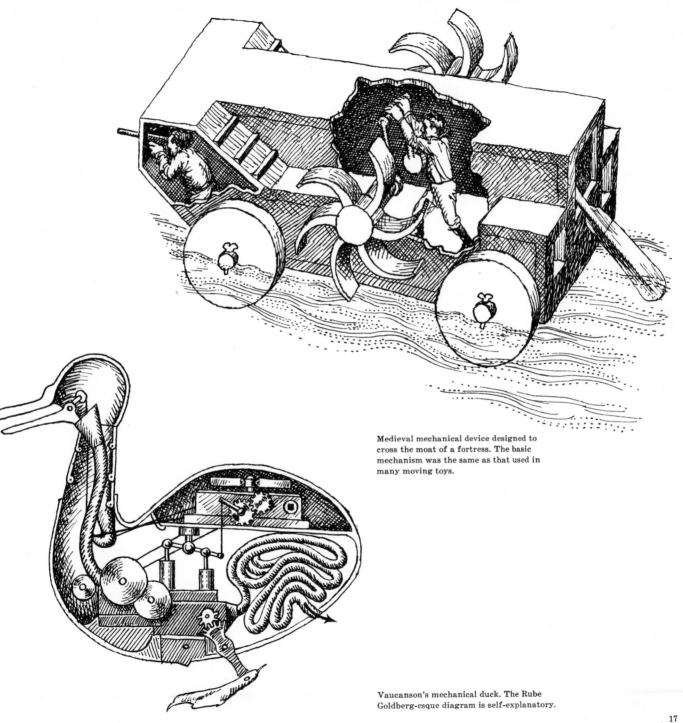

Medieval mechanical device designed to cross the moat of a fortress. The basic mechanism was the same as that used in many moving toys.

Vaucanson's mechanical duck. The Rube Goldberg-esque diagram is self-explanatory.

17

Inside view of a contemporary wind-up robot with an electric bell.

الساقی

American toy auto. Cast iron.

Contemporary toy auto with author's cutout figure.

Opposite Page.
The supreme mechanical toy.
(Collection unknown.)

Classical tin toy soldier.

Moving-eye clock made in Japan. (Collection of the author.)

Donald Duck becomes a glowing toy as a night light. (Collection of the author.)

Vintage Mickey Mouse. Top of a railroad car. (Collection of the author.)

Contemporary Japanese toy engines with author's wooden toy.

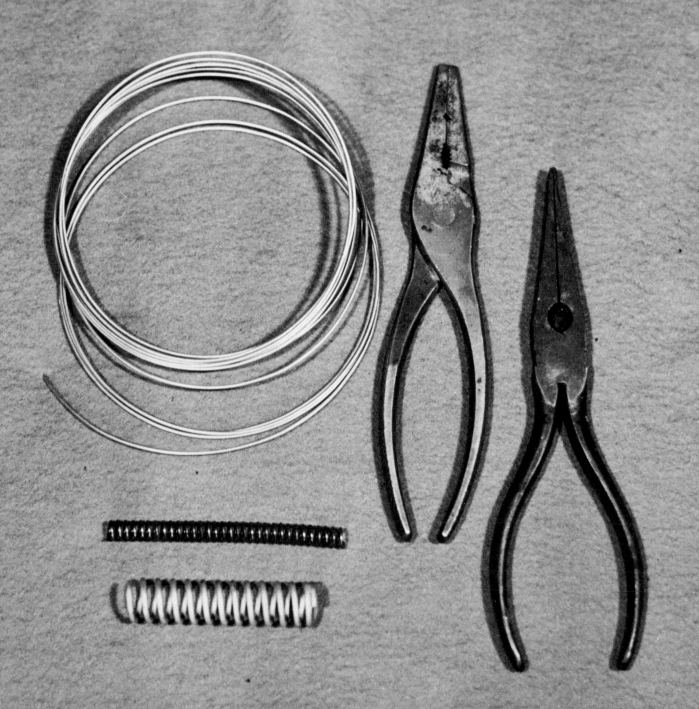

2.

Wire Sculpture, Moving and Non-moving

The toy sculptures in this chapter were constructed with very simple materials: wire (18 gauge, galvanized), small steel springs, and a variety of "found" objects, such as beads, chains, buttons, combs, eyeglasses, fabric, etc. With the exception of the soldering equipment, the tools are equally simple: pliers, wire cutters, screwdriver and small screws. The electric soldering tool costs just a few dollars. Solder is bought in rolls. Except for the found objects, which are free for the taking from your own pocket or the trash can, everything listed can be purchased at a hardware store. A note about soldering: Be sure the pieces to be joined are clean. Apply heat with the electric soldering tool to both surfaces or joints; then apply the solder. It will adhere to both surfaces, joining them.

Even though the materials are inexpensive and simple, they can produce beautiful three-dimensional constructions when they are combined with wit and inventiveness. Wire is easy to shape; it can be worked into bold, easy, flowing lines or manipulated with the fingers and pliers into complicated patterns. Wire sculpture is a wonderful technique for learning to work with space as a major design element. It is really drawing in three dimensions. As the piece (or the spectator) moves, lines and suggested shapes continually realign themselves. Moving toy sculptures provide a uniquely satisfying experience for the contemporary craftsman and student because they encourage him to work in a creative and original way with time and space — the most compelling forces of the twentieth century.

The basic materials for wire sculpture include pliers, wire cutters, wire, springs (for moving sculpture), and solder and soldering tool (not shown).

The following demonstration shows the construction of a simple moving wire sculpture. The five steps illustrated here are basic to the development of almost any wire sculpture, moving or non-moving.

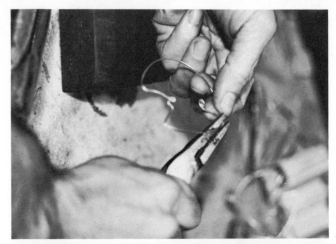

1. The simple head-shape of one of the figures is formed from wire using fingers and pliers.

2. One of the two figures that make up the final piece is finished. Head, arms, and sword have been soldered to a steel spring torso. The "legs" are soldered to the bottom of the spring. In this illustration, the figure (shown upside-down) has just been soldered to the wire crossbar.

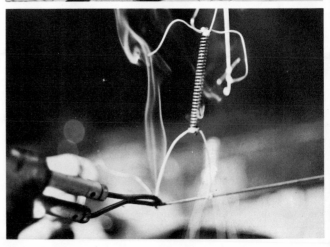

3. The second figure is finished and is being soldered to the opposite end of the crossbar.

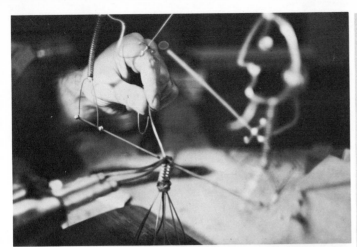

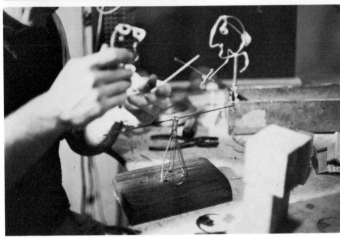

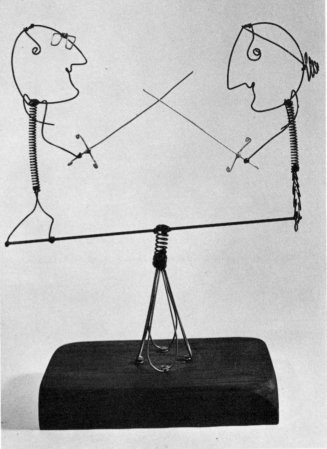

4. Here the crossbar supporting the two jousting figures is being soldered onto the steel base spring. The base is made up of four wire loops which are soldered to the base spring and screwed onto a wooden block.

5. The figures are given a final adjustment to assure a perfect balance.

6. Dueling Couple. The finished wire sculpture "duels" back and forth when touched.

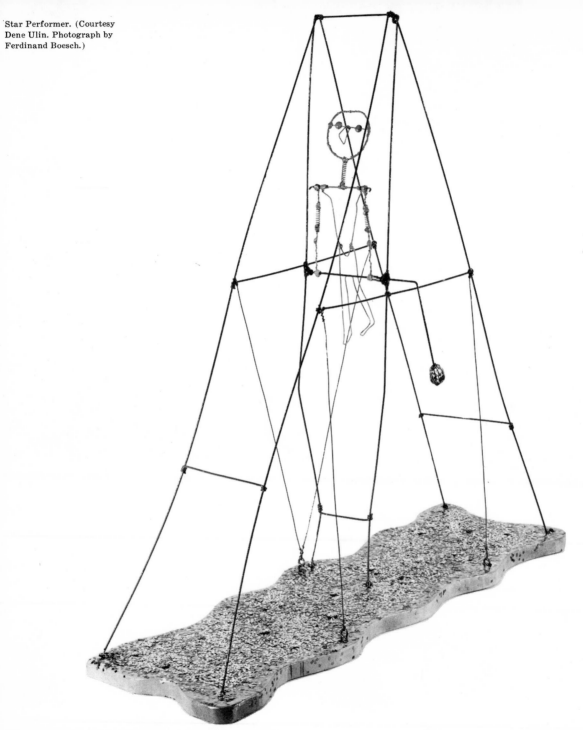

Star Performer. (Courtesy Dene Ulin. Photograph by Ferdinand Boesch.)

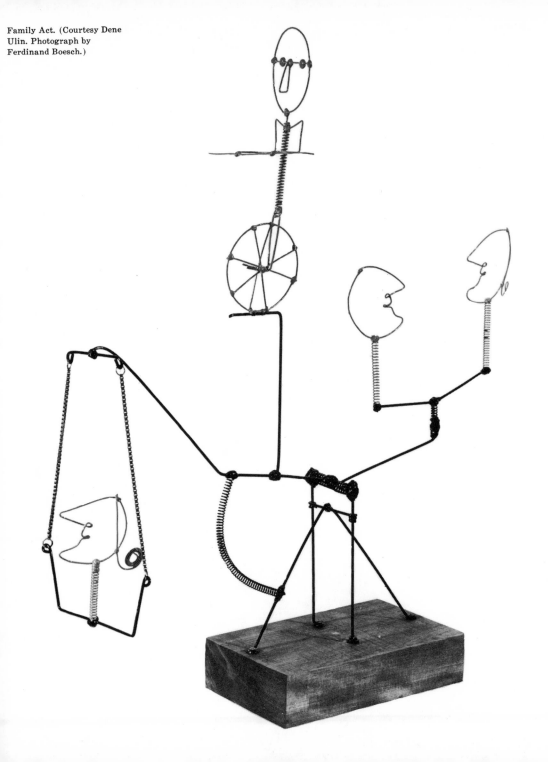

Family Act. (Courtesy Dene
Ulin. Photograph by
Ferdinand Boesch.)

School Mate.

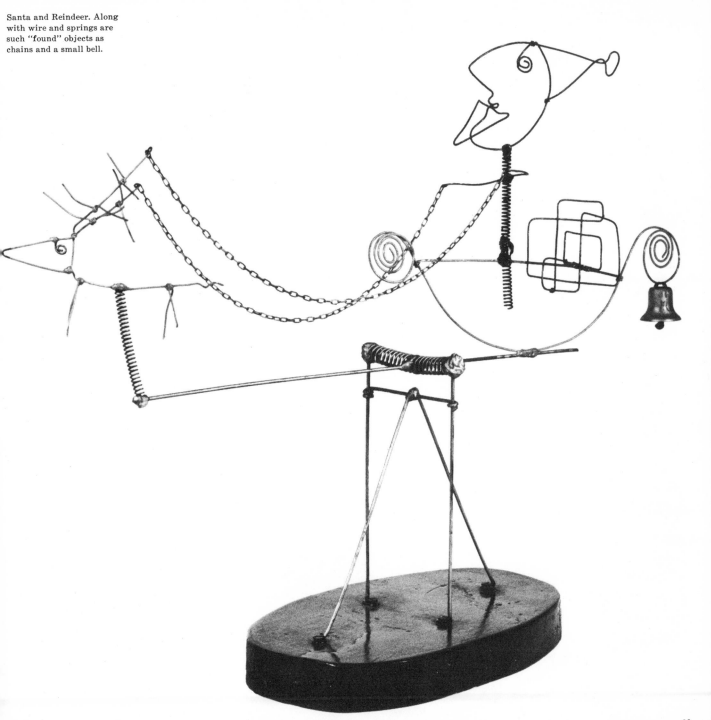

Santa and Reindeer. Along with wire and springs are such "found" objects as chains and a small bell.

Lady Sampler. Found objects include metal mesh net, eyeglasses, beads and fabric. (Collection Renita Hanfling.)

Duel-It-Yourself Knight. Wire and steel spring mounted on a wooden block. The extra sword is for the observer who wants to try his luck with the knight.

Picasso Chick.

Lady Pearl. Beaded fabric, eyeglasses, and metal chain are incorporated in this sculpture. (Collection of Lee Epstein.)

Mr. Black. (Photograph by Ferdinand Boesch.)

Old Mainliner.

King David as a Boy. The harp is made of fine-gauge wire. The eyes are coins; the hair, costume jewelry; and the crown is an antique silver-mounted comb. (Photograph by Ferdinand Boesch.)

Left
Looking Glass Princess. A
whimsical — but aristocratic
— image composed of a
small hand mirror, pieces of
costume jewelry, and fabric.

Castle of Cards and Blocks. The
alphabet blocks and playing cards
(of paper not coated in plastic) are
glued together with Elmer's white
emulsion glue.

Uncle Sam as a Young Man. (Costume
created with Clydeen Malloch.
Photograph by Ferdinand Boesch.)

St. George and the Dragon.

In the sculptures that follow found objects play a dominant role. To the imaginative mind of the artist-craftsman, almost any common object — salt shaker, keys, spoon, clock works, playing card — assumes a whimsical life of its own. The step-by-step demonstration on pps. 46-47 shows the construction of a shield and staff-bearing knight from a spoon and pocket watch parts.

2. 3.

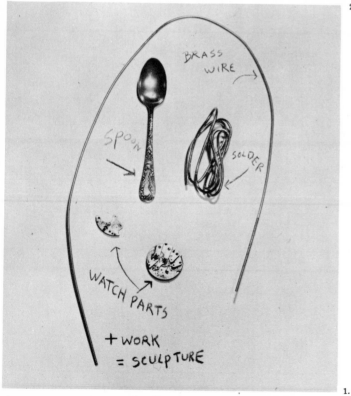

1.

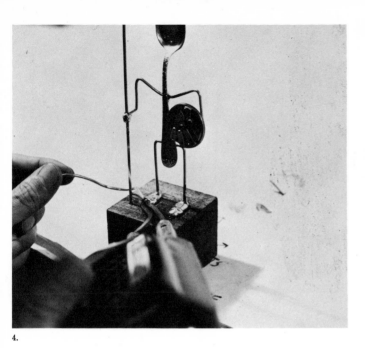

4.

5.

CONSTRUCTING A SCULPTURE FROM FOUND OBJECTS

1. The parts of the figure — spoon and wire — are assembled.

2. Arms and legs are joined to the torso with the electric soldering tool and soldering wire.

3. The watch-part shield is soldered to an arm.

4. Feet are formed by a continuous application of solder. The sculpture has been affixed to the wooden base block with screws. The staff is soldered to the figure's right hand.

5. The finished toy sculpture.

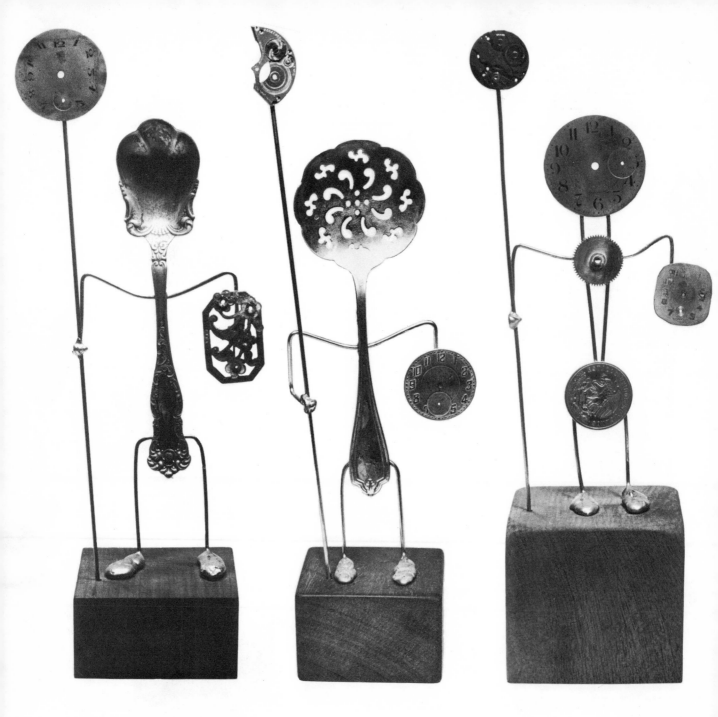

Silver Knight.   Salad Knight.   Watch Knight. (Collection Anthony Murad.)

Gone Knight.

Exchequer. (Courtesy Dene Ulin.)

All Knight. Salt shaker and bits of costume jewelry.

Swinging Clock. A mobile approach to telling time using miscellaneous watch works.

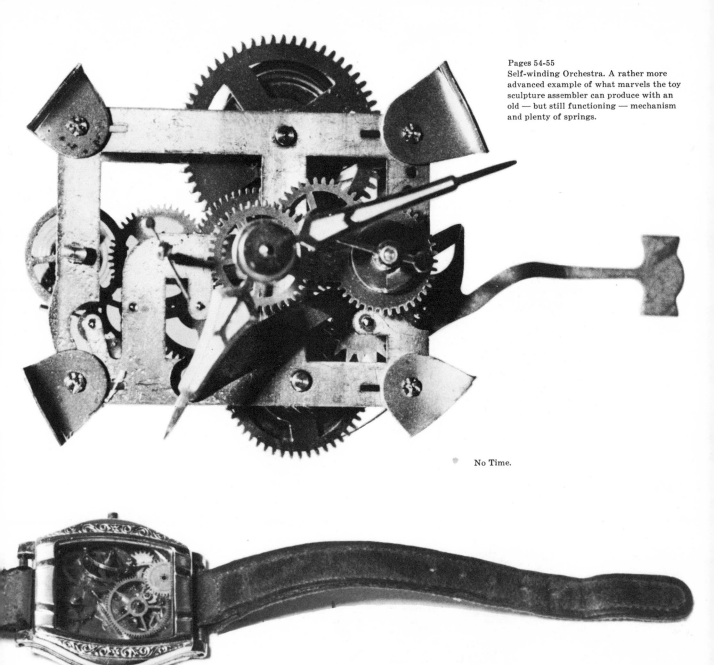

Pages 54-55
Self-winding Orchestra. A rather more
advanced example of what marvels the toy
sculpture assembler can produce with an
old — but still functioning — mechanism
and plenty of springs.

No Time.

Play Watch.

Looking Glass Princess. A whimsical — but aristocratic — image composed of a small hand mirror, pieces of costume jewelry, and fabric.

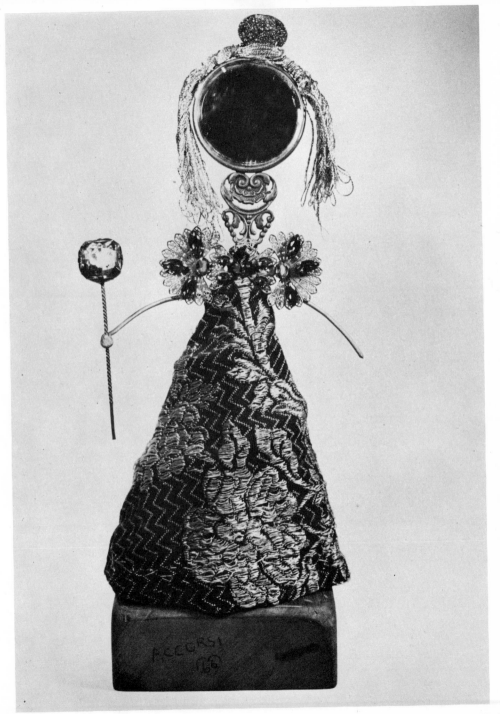

Opposite Page
Above. Jig-cut plywood figures.
Below. King's Exchequer.

Time Exposed. An assemblage of clock
parts mounted on wood, reminiscent of
nineteenth-century still life.

Toy Prince. Bits of scrap wood are joined with screws and white glue.

Castle of Cards and Blocks. The alphabet blocks and playing cards (of paper not coated in plastic) are glued together with Elmer's white emulsion glue.

Clock with Thirteen Hours. The clock face is made of lengths of wire and found objects soldered together; the shaft and base of a wooden newell post and block.

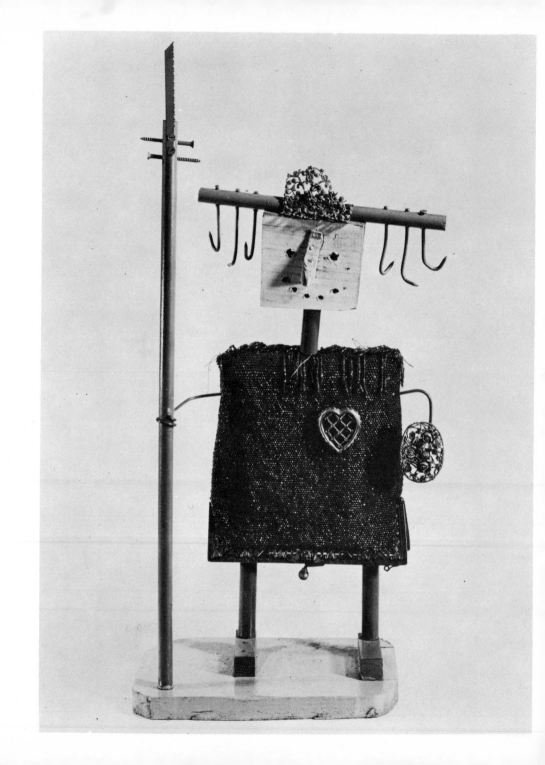

Happy Warrior. This soulful
assemblage incorporates a
beaded bag, costume jewelry,
and fish hooks.

Christ Stilling the Waters. Ship and free-form waves are pieces of wood screwed together and painted. The disciples sport fabric tunics on their wire frames.

3.

Wooden Cut-out Sculpture

The toy sculptures illustrated in this chapter were cut out with a small, inexpensive jig saw. Because of its rapid cutting and easy manipulation, the jig saw encourages spontaneity in design and execution. The wood used here was primarily ¼-inch pine; however, wood scraps of almost any size and thickness will do. Unusual pieces will often suggest interesting cutouts.

Sometimes the figures were sketched on the wood before they were cut out; others were designed as they were cut on the jig saw with no preliminary planning at all. Most of the sculptures were joined with white emulsion glue only. Nails or screws are seldom required on small, light pieces. The wooden cut-out sculptures were painted with watercolor wash, permitting the wood grain to show through.

(Photograph by Ellen Keusch.)

Pentagon Inspection. The figures on
horseback are constructed of six separate
pieces glued together.

Opposite Page
Adam and Eve as Royalty.

Do.

Re.

Mi.

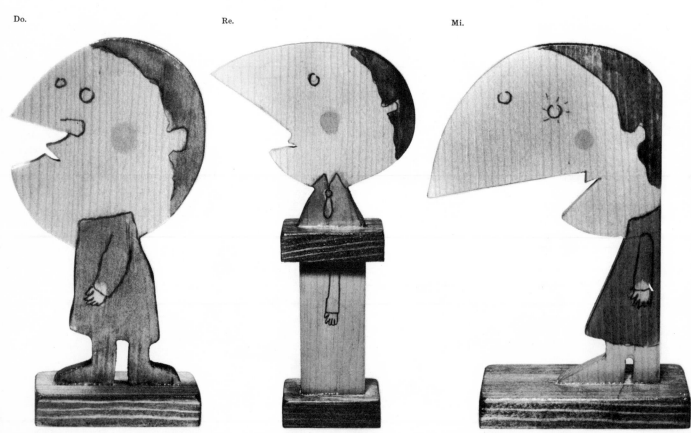

Opposite Page
Spools can be used with or
without thread as building
parts in wooden cutouts.

Fa.

Everyone's Hero.

Sol.

Opposite Page
Board Meeting.

Instant Hero.

Favorite Toy. The wood pieces are screwed together and varnished. Found objects are used for sword, tail, and bridle. The wheels are made of spool tops.

Nutshell Library. Slip cases for miniature books, alphabet blocks, and found items.

Robin Hood.
(Collection Grace
George Alexander.)

Teddy Bear Knight.
(Photograph by
Ferdinand Boesch.)

4.

A Portfolio of Toys by Artists

So much of contemporary art and craft embodies a "serious" and tortured quality that some artists who still manage an ironic view of things have turned their talents to the small-scale, playful world of toy sculpture.

In November, 1963, the Museum of Contemporary Crafts of the American Craftsmen's Council, New York, unveiled the first major show of toys by an artist. During that same time the Betty Parsons Gallery held a group show of toys by artists. Both of these exhibits received a great deal of public attention and acclaim. In December, 1964, the Museum of Contemporary Crafts presented a show of toys featuring the work of professional artists and children.

At a time of overwhelming — and burdensome — technological progress and proliferation of flashy material goods, there is something perversely pleasing about objects made for pure enjoyment — and often of junk.

(Photograph by John Chernoble.)

CARL A. RUDISILL LIBRARY
LENOIR RHYNE COLLEGE

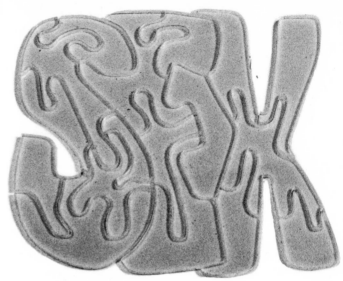

Sex by Betty Thomson. Plastic word puzzle.
(Photograph by Renita Hanfling.)

Left
Charlie Chaplin by Jacqueline Fogel. Polychrome
wood. (Collection of Mel May and Vernon P.
Becker, New York. Photograph by Polaris Pictures
Inc.)

Bottom
Rocking Horse by Don Drumm. Moving parts of
cast and welded aluminum.

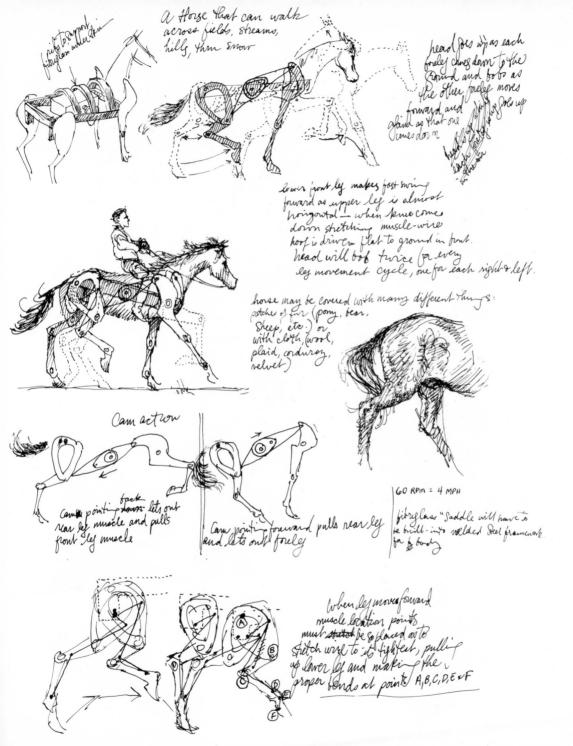

A Horse that can walk across fields, streams, hills, thru snow

pipes to support fibreglass outer skin

head goes up as each foreleg comes down to the ground and bobs as the other foreleg moves forward and down so that one comes down

lower front leg makes foot swing forward as upper leg is almost horizontal — when knee comes down stretching muscle-wire hoof is driven flat to ground in front. head will bob twice for every leg movement cycle, one for each right & left.

horse may be covered with many different things: patches of fur (pony, bear, sheep, etc.) or with cloth (wool, plaid, corduroy, velvet)

Cam action

Cam pointing back lets out rear leg muscle and pulls front leg muscle

Cam pointing forward pulls rear leg and lets out foreleg

60 RPM = 4 MPH

fibreglass "saddle will have to be built into welded steel framework for the body

When leg moves forward muscle location points must be so placed as to stretch wire to its tightest, pulling up lower leg and making the proper bends at points A, B, C, D, E & F

Preliminary Studies for Walking Horse by Edward Epstein.

83

Two Figures by Mary Gordon.
(Photograph by Peter
Orlando.)

Acrobats by Earl Krentzin. Silver on ivory.
Balancing toy.